Discovering Melbourne's fir... hide-and-seek. Though it doesn't h... some Australian cities, it is the co... quiet charm that lies in i...

Brunch is a religion here and the gems in this storied town are, often found down nondescript laneways. It's certainly not a destination where checkboxes are ticked off, but a place that requires years to truly get to know. There's a story behind each piece of street art, unique one-of-a-kind wares in retail shops and a fiery pursuit of innovation in every famed kitchen.

It's that independent spirit, coupled with scenic drives and cultural and sporting events, that makes Melbourne a worthy visit. Soak up the stunning vistas at the Great Ocean Road one afternoon, and cheer at a tennis or AFL final the next. Wander into hole-in-the-walls and embrace the experience. Melbourne still surprises me every single day.

amelia chia
writer

Amelia Chia is a writer and editor whose work has appeared in international publications including *Harper's BAZAAR, Elle, Buro 24/7 Singapore* and *The Collective*. Born in Singapore, she now resides in Melbourne after getting hitched to a hipster Melburnian. When not burying her nose behind a laptop or keeping up with social media trends, she can be found indulging in one of her four main interests – fashion, beauty, food and travel.

sayher heffernan
photographer

With a love for intimate and honest visual storytelling, Sayher Heffernan is found most weekends at a wedding, camera in hand. However, his eye for detail and love for light extends beyond weddings. He's also worked with established companies such as kikki.K, Food & Desire, Studio Brave and Sonelo Design Studio, shooting everything from architectural interiors to portraits and food.

where to lay your weary head

Rest up, relax and recharge

COPPERSMITH

COPPERSMITH

Home away from home

435 Clarendon Street (near Thomson Street; South Melbourne)
+61 3 8696 7777 / coppersmithhotel.com.au
Double from AU$230

Formerly the Cricket Club Hotel, Coppersmith was given a makeover in 2014 and now boasts 15 polished guestrooms. From the sleek pendant lights to the attractive parquet flooring, this boutique hotel has created a cosmopolitan space that feels like your own. I love how impeccable the service is here – all you have to do is ask and the team will go all out to recommend the best eats, shops and even the nearest yoga studio. If you feel like staying in, pop down to Coppersmith Bar and Bistro for pub grub and craft brews.

ST JEROME'S THE HOTEL

QT MELBOURNE

The definitive trendsetter

133 Russell Street (near Portland Lane; CBD) / +61 3 8636 8800
qthotelsandresorts.com/Melbourne
Double from AU$290

QT Melbourne is all about sensory perfection. The contemporary digs are filled with quirky art pieces, including a towering stack of old paperbacks stuffed into a wall. Each room is fitted out in a bold color scheme with sophisticated touches, such as patterned wardrobe wallpaper and Japanese-inspired sliding doors. At sundown, the QT Rooftop Bar is the only place to be: grab a couple of cocktails (the Yarra Valley Sour is my jam) and tasty sliders, then enjoy the glittering view of the CBD. For dinner, head down to swanky Euro-bistro Pascale Bar & Grill, which serves up hearty dishes, including a beautiful selection of wood-fired meats. But my favorite part? The elevators, one of which told me I look better from behind. Programmed to say over 50 tongue-in-cheek phrases, they detect the amount of people and call out accordingly.

ST JEROME'S THE HOTEL

Luxury glamping

Level 3, 271 Little Lonsdale Street (near Elizabeth Street; CBD)
+61 4 0611 8561 / stjeromesthehotel.com.au
Double from AU$420

If you're looking for a unique stay, this is it.
St Jerome's The Hotel opulent camping on a rooftop with the city skyline acting as the backdrop. Each of the 21 canvas-bell tents comes with a double or queen bed, plush robes, a split system air-conditioner, a portable cooler with complimentary beers and ciders, and a tablet loaded with movies. As for the bathrooms, there are nine chic facilities that are stocked with luxurious ASPAR hand soap, moisturizer, shampoo and conditioner. What's more, the rate includes a beverage per person, tea delivery before bed and a breakfast box with fresh coffee in the morning.

THE LYALL

Quiet enclave

16 Murphy Street (near Toorak Road; South Yarra) / +61 3 9868 8222
thelyall.com
Double from AU$230

Located in a tranquil, upscale neighborhood, The Lyall is an elegant option for those who prefer being away from the buzz of the city, but still close to superb lifestyle options: this high-end accommodation is a short walk away from tons of boutiques and eateries on Chapel Street. There are only 40 one- and two-bedroom suites on this property, and each is wonderfully spacious, featuring stately floor to ceiling windows that open to a private balcony.

THE PRINCE

Beachside sophistication

2 Acland Street (near Fitzroy Street; St Kilda) / +61 3 9536 1111
theprince.com.au
Double from AU$175

Sumptuous and elegant, The Prince overlooks the waters of Port Phillip Bay in the heart of St Kilda. It's like being in Melbourne's version of balmy Los Angeles – step out of the lobby and you're inhaling the salty sea air. The rooms are bathed in natural light and boast a neutral color palette with exclusive touches, such as neatly-folded throws and light fixtures created from craypots. Tip: don't forget to book in at the award-winning Aurora Spa (see pg 106) before checking out.

fitzroy and collingwood

Just two kilometers (about one mile) northeast of the city center, lie Fitzroy and Collingwood, Melbourne's oldest suburbs. Littered with a blend of stylish and quirky shops, these enclaves are inner-city meccas for vintage shopping, secondhand bookstores, record shops, local fashion labels and independent home goods. I love people-watching here – on weekends, buskers fill the air with music as an eclectic crowd takes to the streets. Food and dining options here are equally limitless: there are classy bars, Mexican taquerias, rooftop tapas, great vegetarian joints and the occasional fine-dining spot. My usual route includes four roads full of smashing options that are simple to navigate: I hit up Gertrude Street, make a right onto Brunswick Street, continue over to Johnston Street and finally make my way down Smith Street. Enjoy!

1 Christian Kimber
2 Cutler & Co
3 George's Bar
4 Industry Beans
5 Le Bon Ton
6 Lightly
7 Loose Leaf

8 Lune Croissanterie
9 Modern Times
10 The Everleigh
11 The Rose St Artists' Market
12 Third Drawer Down
13 Zetta Florence

CHRISTIAN KIMBER

Sneaker obsession

264 Johnston Street (near Smith Street) / +61 3 9486 9690
christiankimber.com / Closed Mondays

Looking for artisan-crafted men's shoes with a streetwear edge? This is the place. The London-born, Melbourne-based Christian Kimber learned the ropes of classically constructed footwear around Savile Row before moving to Australia in 2011. His Fitzroy store is most aptly described as hipster meets haute – the first thing you'll see is a gorgeous gold sign before entering this haven of shiny pebble flooring and wares propped on raw logs. Focusing on high-quality kicks, the majority of his goods are made in a small town just outside Florence, Italy. I'm all about white kicks for gents at the moment, so the Lower Fifth Mid-Top in White Grain is my pick.

One of the things I love most about the restaurant scene here is that you can get a mind-blowingly fantastic, upscale meal without burning a hole in your pocket. Cutler & Co is one such place – its fare is definitively modern Australian, and includes the finesse and attention to detail that chef Andrew McConnell is known for. The roasted flounder entrée is high on my priority list whenever I visit because the skin is crisped to perfection. If you're in a group, I urge you to share the dry aged 1.1kg (2.5lbs) O'Connor rib-eye. This tender, charred beauty is a meat lover's dream, served with a side of cabbage and fennel salad for sweet relief.

Themed bars always have me envisioning kitsch, but when it comes to George's Bar – a tribute to neurotic *Seinfeld* character George Costanza – that's just not the case. Aside from the signed pilot script, this pub champions a no-frills attitude, and is decked out in murals by local artists Adnate and Shawn Lu and a selection of art given to them by their patrons. Sink your teeth into one of their toasties while sipping on a signature libation. My usual is The Quitter sandwich – basil pesto, tomato and mozzarella – followed by The Pie Guy, a sweet mix of vodka, apple liqueur, moonshine, cinnamon syrup, egg white and topped with a burnt cinnamon stick and an apple slice. Otherwise, grab a beer and go nuts on the Twix machine or Frogger arcade game.

INDUSTRY BEANS

Industrial-cool brunch

3/62 Rose Street (near Fitzroy Street) / +61 3 9417 1034
industrybeans.com / Open daily

In a place like Fitzroy, the prime establishments are found tucked down
back streets and laneways. Industry Beans is no different, but when you find
the open warehouse, it's like chancing upon a sacred rectangle of buzzing
chatter and warm camaraderie. The high ceilings and cute, open-air front
yard emit a welcoming vibe. Food here is progressive and seasonal, making
use of the freshest produce there is on offer at the time. Your must-try?
The shanklish cheese omelet. It's a superb balance of sweet and savory,
with Middle Eastern-spiced cow's cheese, caramelized leeks, za'atar,
beetroot and kale on a thick slice of sourdough toast.

LE BON TON

Cajun smokehouse

51 Gipps Street (near Rokeby Street) / +61 3 9416 4341
lebonton.com.au / Open daily

Fried chicken, beef brisket and mac and cheese are some of life's most marvelous things, and that's why Le Bon Ton is pretty hard to resist. This New Orleans-inspired bistro and bar, run by brothers Will and Mick Balleau, is all for hearty flavors. Kick off with a smooth Sazerac, followed by the abovementioned trio and their "kitchen sink" salad to share. I'm not one to advocate a salad unless it's truly worth it, and this is one of the best I've tried. A blend of iceberg and red oak lettuce, cucumber, tomato, red onion, smoked cheddar and tortilla strips tossed with a tasty chipotle ranch dressing is in one word: amazing.

LIGHTLY

Housewares with a story

3 Glasshouse Road (near Wellington Street) / +61 3 9417 2440
lightly.com.au / Closed Sunday

I could happily spend an entire day in Lightly. Shopping here is like walking into a good friend's home — it smells heavenly and the staff is always happy to answer any questions you might have. Established in 2005 by Cindy-Lee Davies as a tribute to her grandmother, Rosemary Estelle Lightly, this incredible shop is thoughtfully stocked with functional home goods inspired by a sense of adventure and resourcefulness. Whether it's classic planters made from powder-coated spun metal, terracotta ceramics or light fixtures that reference the moon, Lightly stays true to its usage of innovative materials. I always find myself gravitating toward the hanging planters and selection of Normann Copenhagen products. But, can you blame me?

LOOSE LEAF

Industrial jungle

31 Sackville Street (near Budd Street) / +61 3 9994 6865
looseleafstore.com.au / Open Thursday through Saturday

Loose Leaf's photogenic botanical design studio is unlike your average florist atelier or plant store. Located in a converted warehouse, the interior resembles an indoor rainforest, and is both a shop and a work space for owners Charlie Lawler and Wona Bae to create horticultural installations. This imaginative pair wanted a place where they could get creative and connect with nature, and they certainly have. From monstera chandeliers to hip fiddle-leaf figs, there's no lack of choice. You'll want to arrange your next home around their luscious foliage.

LUNE CROISSANTERIE

Pastry heaven

119 Rose Street (near Young Street) / +61 3 9419 2320
lunecroissanterie.com / Open Thursday through Monday

This is my usual pit-stop for Melbourne's superlative croissants. Housed in an old factory, sibling pair Kate and Cam Reid have designed two ways to enjoy this experience: join the line for the main service counter, or book and pre-pay online for one of the nine stools in the Lune Lab glass cube, where you're served three courses of pastries (including two plates that aren't on the regular menu) and unlimited coffee. No matter which option you go for, you need to try the Reuben, a savory croissant with pastrami, sauerkraut, Swiss cheese and Russian dressing. But if it's a sweet treat you're after, the twice-baked carrot cake is actually a croissant that features spiced walnut, carrot frangipane and cream cheese frosting.

MODERN TIMES

A slice of Denmark

311 Smith Street (near Perry Street) / **+61 3 9913 8598**
moderntimes.com.au / **Open daily**

Amy and Joel Malin have impeccable taste in furniture and design,
and if you happen to be walking past their expansive store on
Smith Street, this fact is readily apparent. The power couple sources
teak and rosewood furnishings from Denmark and other parts of
Europe, as well as original artwork from acclaimed Australian artists.
I love how meticulously curated the store is – dig deep and you'll
find pretty ceramics, textiles and jewelry styled alongside the home
décor. It's a tip-top place to pick up a gift for an artsy friend and it will
certainly get your design juices flowing. I always leave wishing I could
afford to re-do my entire living room.

THE EVERLEIGH

Swanky speakeasy

150-156 Gertrude Street (near Napier Street) / +61 3 9416 2229
theeverleigh.com / Open daily

This classy bar is a haven for hooch insiders in need of a stiff drink.
Designed to recall a 1920s hideaway – complete with live music playing
on certain lucky nights – gentlemen in suits and ladies in little black
dresses are a dime a dozen here. There's a straightforward cocktail menu
that showcases all the usual Prohibition-Era suspects, but if you're feeling
adventurous, tell the bartender your preferred fruits, flavors and spirits
and you'll soon have your very own dream libation. I adore their version of
The Penicillin, a smoky, spicy twist on a whisky sour made with peated
whisky, blended Scotch, fresh ginger, honey water and garnished with
candied ginger. It gets me all the time, every time.

THE ROSE ST. ARTISTS' MARKET

Treasure trove

60 Rose Street (near Fitzroy Street) / +61 3 9419 5529
rosestmarket.com.au / Open Saturday and Sunday

The Rose St. Artists' Market is a tucked-away outlet that is synonymous with Melbourne's creative scene. Inspired by Brooklyn's DUMBO Collective, I love that emerging artists and designers have come together to showcase their crafts here and that I can always count on finding amazing wares, such as whimsical furniture, intricate jewelry and original paintings. Come with a full wallet and an intrepid spirit – I've never been able to leave empty-handed and I hope the same goes for you.

THIRD DRAWER DOWN

Eclectic finds

93 George Street (near Gertrude Street) / +61 3 9534 4088
thirddrawerdown.com / Open daily

When I'm looking for a present or a little something to inspire, this is
where I know I can procure it. Third Drawer Down is an independent
concept destination that is populated with objects from all around the
world. Calling themselves a retailer, wholesaler and design studio, this airy,
light-filled shop is like a gallery of sorts, where niche objects, housewares,
books and jewelry are beautifully displayed on shelves and in drawers. With
a focus on illustration and print design, expect sweet wares from artists like
Ai Weiwei, Sam Francis and Yayoi Kusama.

ZETTA FLORENCE

Fine parchment and gifts

97B Brunswick Street (near Moor Street) +61 3 9039 5583
zettaflorence.com.au **Open daily**

I get lost in my own thoughts in Zetta Florence. With good reason: there's so much to take in. Founded in 1989, this expansive, family-run business specializes in premium handmade paper, photo albums, leather-bound journals and other gorgeous stationery like printed cards, calendars and boxes. Some of the images found on the goods are from photo collections shot within Australia, but others are sourced from different parts of the world to fit in with the shop's retro-chic signature style. There's nothing like spending hours thumbing through bits and bobs you never knew you needed.

top shots

Convenient coffee on the go

BURNSIDE
87A Smith Street (near Gertrude Street; Fitzroy)
+61 3 8394 7335, no website, open daily

EVERYDAY MIDTOWN
213 Little Collins Street (near Athenaeum Place;
CBD), no phone, no website, closed Sunday

MAKER FINE COFFEE
47 North Street (near Vaughan Street; Richmond)
No phone, makerfinecoffee.com
closed Sunday and Monday

MARKET LANE COFFEE
176 Faraday Street (near Drummond Street; Carlton)
+61 3 9804 7434, marketlane.com.au, open daily

PATRICIA COFFEE BREWERS
Corner of Little Bourke & Little William Streets (CBD)
+61 3 9642 2237, patriciacoffee.com.au
Closed Saturday and Sunday

Melburnians are accustomed to erratic four-seasons-in-a-day weather, but an inconsistent mug in this coffee capital is equivalent to having a truly dreary day. There's no such thing as "I'd like a coffee, please" – your request would elicit blank stares – so knowing exactly what you want before you order will give you local status. Here are five fail-safe joints that serve up a mean flat white and long black.

Patricia Coffee Brewers is a no-frills, standing-room only institution hidden amidst towering corporate buildings in the CBD. Reminiscent of European coffee bars, this isn't a place to sit and have long chats, but if you are after a deliciously smooth java, you'll get it here. Owner Bowen Holden offers a house blend as well as a single origin from local roaster Seven Seeds, and his knowledgeable team are always happy to explain anything to you.

Down the middle of the CBD is **Everyday Midtown**. While the original outpost in Collingwood encourages people to linger over black filter coffees, co-owner Mark Free has designed this location to be a takeaway destination. I enjoy purposeful strolls here, ordering over the polished-concrete bar and people-watching as I wait. Their banana bread is pretty legit, too.

Burnside is the cute corner shop in Fitzroy everyone notices when they drive past. Located at the junction of Smith and Gertrude Streets, the floor-to-ceiling windows inspire peeks into its bright, open space. There's no pretense here, just a cracking cup of joe with beans by Seven Seeds and sandwiches to-go.

Dedicated to high-quality brews, **Market Lane Coffee** is Melbourne's very own speciality roaster, café and retailer. They source beans from some of the world's first-rate coffee growers and aim for a distinctive taste in each mug. I'm a sucker for their flat white as it's rich, fragrant and not overly acidic; plus, it pairs nicely with buttered toast and fruit jam.

Tucked away amongst factories and warehouses in Richmond is **Maker Fine Coffee**, a hole-in-the-wall coffee bar that brews some of the best single origins and blends from Kenya, Colombia and Ethiopia. One for the true connoisseur, they do an incredible Kenyan pour-over – it made my taste buds tingle with its bold fruit sweetness and syrupy finish.

carlton and north melbourne

Anchored by Italian restaurants, wine stores, pubs and boutiques, the streets of Carlton are a diverse mix of sights and scents, and a small reflection of what it used to be back in the day. The main thoroughfare, Lygon Street, was a Jewish neighborhood up until the 1940s. After WWII, Italian immigrants took over and the area became alternative and bohemian, with a rich theater and film influence – today, the iconic Cinema Nova still attracts culture vultures with its screenings of arthouse films. I'm always impressed at how alive this place is on the weekends – you'll find throngs of people dining outdoors on the sidewalks of Lygon and Faraday Streets. During winter, one of my very favorite things to do is check out hot chocolate slingers, and a good number are located here, as well as in its slightly under-the-radar neighbor, North Melbourne. I find both hoods completely marvelous because on any day I can nosh on cuisine ranging from classic Italian to experimental Thai-Australian, and then hit up lively vintage shops right across the road.

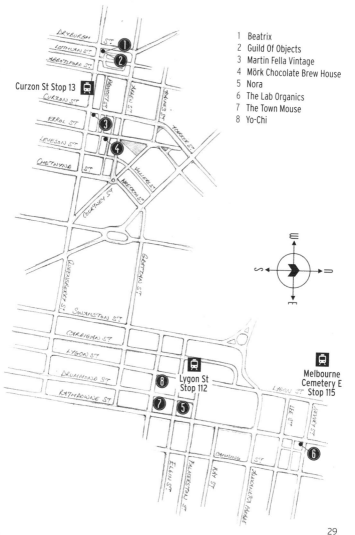

1 Beatrix
2 Guild Of Objects
3 Martin Fella Vintage
4 Mörk Chocolate Brew House
5 Nora
6 The Lab Organics
7 The Town Mouse
8 Yo-Chi

Curzon St Stop 13

Lygon St Stop 112

Melbourne Cemetery E Stop 115

BEATRIX

Honest, old-fashioned confections

**688 Queensberry Street (near Dryburgh Street) / +61 4 0369 8836
beatrixbakes.com / Closed Sunday and Monday**

This is exactly the kind of bakery I love. It's tiny and charmingly retro with confections like ciabatta rolls, sweet pies, cookies, lamingtons and, of course, their incredible cakes displayed on white, tiered stands and floral plates. There's no neon sign or marble tables, no drips or edible flowers – just the tastiest gateau I've had in Melbourne. Each slice is huge and can easily be shared between two (or three!) people. Their red velvet is my dessert ideal: exceptionally moist and layered with a white chocolate cream cheese for an unbelievable balance of flavor.

GUILD OF OBJECTS

Artist collective

690 Queensberry Street (near Dryburgh Street) / +61 4 3264 7445
guildofobjects.com / Open Wednesday through Saturday

Art and design lovers, rejoice. This fabulous emporium brings together
a new generation of Australian makers, crafters, artists and artisans in
one stunning collection that is incredibly hard to resist. Each piece is
delightfully one-of-a-kind; whether it's a serving bowl by Barbara McIvor,
a copper spoon by Kat Relish, a vase with its own story or a handmade scarf,
everything seems to call out to my wallet. Come visit, and be prepared to
leave surprised.

MARTIN FELLA VINTAGE

Refinement defined

556 Queensberry Street (near Queensberry Place) / +61 4 1164 1269
facebook.com/martin.fella.vintage / Closed Sunday and Monday

Nearly twenty years after Martin Fella opened the doors of his eponymous secondhand shop, he still feels no need for an e-commerce website. "Online shopping? If the world was all about that, it would be such a boring place," he says. I love walking in here and having a chat with Martin, who relishes a passionate conversation about fashion. This gem isn't your ordinary pre-owned shop where clothes smell musky and feel like hand-me-downs. The store is stylish and well-curated, featuring haute labels like Celine, Louis Vuitton, Marc Jacobs, Scanlan Theodore, Vivienne Westwood and Anglomania. He gets his stock from auctions and sources from all over the world; believe me, the breadth of designs he carries is an incredible sight in itself.

MÖRK CHOCOLATE BREW HOUSE

A real chocolate indulgence

150 Errol Street (near Byron Street) / +61 3 9328 1386
morkchocolate.com.au / Closed Monday

Mörk Chocolate Brew House is bright and cheery — imagine bleached wood, hanging foliage and touches of gold. But as the name suggests, this is a dedicated chocolate haven, so leave other cravings at the door. I normally order their signature campfire chocolate, a stemless glass filled with smoke, a beaker of hot chocolate and a toasted marshmallow, which you then assemble yourself. It's rich and smoky in taste, and not overly sweet: precisely how I prefer it. You should also try the malted hot chocolate; with malt caramel, dehydrated malted meringues and caramel "snow," it's my idea of Christmas in a cup. The attention to detail here is commendable — even their sparkling water is infused with vanilla bean and acts as a delicate palate cleanser.

NORA

Out-of-the-box dining

156 Elgin Street (near Drummond Street) / **+61 3 9041 8644**
noramelbourne.com / **Closed Sunday and Monday**

Nothing excites me more than a meal at Nora. Serving up Thai-influenced, experimental cuisine in their evening degustation sessions, it's a fascinating, playful progression of courses that will tantalize all your senses. Creative husband-and-wife team Sarin Rojanametin and Jean Thamthanakorn's love for their food can be seen in the way they painstakingly create each plate with precision. The clever "Daft Punk Is Playing In My Mouth" dish is actually blue mackerel served under spicy green-chili granita, a slice of compressed watermelon and a black sesame reduction. It sounds weird, but take it all in with a trusting palate and a gung-ho attitude, and it will all — as promised — come together in your mouth.

THE LAB ORGANICS

Holistic beauty

360 Rathdowne Street (near Newry Street) / +61 3 9347 8871
thelaborganics.com.au / Open daily

Many ladies in Melbourne are all for soft, glowing skin and seek out all things natural and organic. The Lab Organics is true to that belief, encouraging a lifestyle without harmful, synthetic chemicals. I don't always need to buy a new skincare product, but even so, I never fail to walk in when I'm in the area for its brilliant natural light, amazing concoction of scents and well-stocked shelves. It's almost as if time stands still when I'm in here, unscrewing and testing every little pot and jar of goodness. From Grown Alchemist to May Lindstrom Skincare to P.F Candle Co., you name it, they've got it.

THE TOWN MOUSE

Neighborhood treasure with contemporary Australian eats

312 Drummond Street (near Faraday Street) / +61 3 9347 3312
townmouse.com.au / Open daily

The Town Mouse has created an intelligent, produce-focused menu that presents its food with modern techniques worthy of a fine-dining salon — but without the pomp that comes along with it. This quiet achiever only wants to be known as a community establishment, as evidenced by its discreet entrance, but its food and the warmth of the team belie that right; it's so popular amongst insiders that you'll need a reservation at least a week in advance. Inside, the furnishings are refreshingly simple: black-and-cream tiled walls and a curved, oak-topped bar run the gamut here. I frequently crave their complimentary sourdough, which is bread is baked in-house and served with a cracking sesame butter. It's hard to pick a favorite plate, but their chicken breast with sour cream, chicory, hazelnut and lavender is not to be missed.

YO-CHI

Trendy froyo joint

194 Faraday Street (near Lygon Street) / +61 3 9347 7130
yochi.com.au / Open daily

When it comes to frozen yogurt, I think Yo-Chi does it best. This homegrown establishment uses quality ingredients from local farmers and suppliers, and is constantly at the forefront of innovative toppings. Just building your treat is an experience in itself. Grab an empty cup, select from their 12 mind-blowing flavors (my go-tos are their signature tart and the salted butterscotch) and complete your creation with nuts, crunches, mochi, brownie bits, popping candy, fruit and a variety of sauces. They charge by weight, so be aware of how much you're piling on – that said, each bite is worth every cent.

brunch done right

First order of the day

ADDICT FOOD & COFFEE
240-242 Johnston Street (at Gore Street; Fitzroy)
+61 3 9415 6420, addictfoodandcoffee.com.au
open daily

BAWA CAFÉ
248 Burwood Road (near Elizabeth Street;
Hawthorn), +61 3 9819 6701, bawacafe.com
open daily

GRAIN STORE
517 Flinders Lane (near Hay Place; CBD)
+61 3 9972 6993, grainstore.com.au, open daily

TALL TIMBER
60 Commercial Road (near Perth Street; Prahran)
+61 3 9510 4111, talltimbercafe.com.au, open daily

TOP PADDOCK
658 Church Street (near Dale Street; Richmond)
+61 3 9429 4332, toppaddockcafe.com, open daily

TOP PADDOCK

Brunch fare is practically synonymous with Melbourne, and no matter what the weather looks like outside, cafés fill the minute day breaks. Whether it's an antioxidant-packed açaí bowl, chili scrambled eggs or breakfast salad, you name it, we've got it.

At **BAWA Café**'s tropical oasis, it's not surprising to find young families parked outside on weekends waiting for a table. Order the potato rösti with braised pork, eggs and a bright green herb hollandaise for a hearty meal, or the Californian superfood salad – which is packed with goodness like quinoa, kale, charred corn, salted ricotta, black turtle beans, goji berries and spicy lime vinaigrette – and a smoothie (I like the Blended Drink #1, made with banana, peanut butter, cacao nibs, honey and almond milk) if you're on a health kick.

Addict Food & Coffee is an institution in Fitzroy. The coconut chia pudding topped with rhubarb, macadamia, fresh strawberries and white chocolate is summery and light. Otherwise, I'm all for the crowd-pleasing corn fritters with Halloumi and poached eggs. Bonus: there are vegan and gluten-free options.

You might have seen **Top Paddock**'s generous blueberry and ricotta hotcake all over Instagram. Drizzled in maple syrup and topped with berries, seeds and cream, this thick, fluffy cake is a refined version of your childhood breakfast and is good for sharing. Coffees come with single-origin options and all of the ingredients are sourced from organic suppliers in Australia.

If you're down the Spencer Street end of the CBD, check in at **Grain Store**. In the kitchen, head chef Ingo Meissner combines his love for traditional European fare with modern techniques and fresh produce. Try the buttermilk brioche French toast – served with a selection of fruit, tiramisu and pistachio, it brings a sensational hit of sweetness and acidity.

The yummiest eggs Benedict in Melbourne are found at rustic **Tall Timber**. The eggs are poached to runny perfection and served with a slab of slow-cooked pork shoulder, Champagne-poached apple, maple bacon and apple cider hollandaise. Carnivores are certainly in for a real treat.

cbd

To an average tourist, Melbourne's central business district, known as the CBD, is a dream. It's where Bourke Street Mall, Chinatown and scores of corporate offices reside. To me, it's a well-planned rectangle that I can spend an entire day lost in as there's the kind of addictive energy that makes you want to delve deeper and discover more. The CBD is home to some of the city's top shops and restaurants — some proudly displayed on the main avenues, others hidden down the most obscure laneways — and it's up to you to make the experience your own. My ideal day starts off on edgy Flinders Lane, where merry bistros and independent fashion labels are just as celebrated as graffitied walls. Next, I head up Swanston Street onto Bourke Street, where shiny store fronts beckon you to enter. Wander into Emporium or the palatial General Post Office-turned-H&M for big city vibes. Tired of walking? All trams within the city are free, so hop on and off as you please.

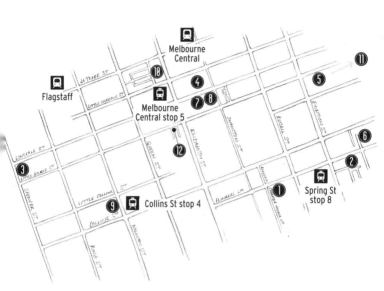

Melbourne
Central

Flagstaff

Melbourne
Central stop 5

Collins St stop 4

Spring St
stop 8

1	Alpha60	7	Metropolis Bookshop
2	Cumulus Inc.	8	Rooftop Cinema
3	High Ground	9	Royal Stacks
4	Incu Store	10	Shortstop Coffee & Donuts
5	Lucy Folk	11	Spring Street Grocer (off map)
6	Mamasita	12	Tipo 00

ALPHA60

Classic clothing in a spectacular space

2nd Floor, Chapter House, 195 Flinders Lane (near Regent Place)
+61 3 9663 3002 / alpha60.com.au / Open daily

Arguably Melbourne's most breathtaking store, Alpha60 is a curator's dream. The second you waltz in you're greeted by magnificent vaulted ceilings, stained-glass windows and a baby grand piano. I've always adored the cuts, fabrics and attention to detail that this local fashion brand is known for, but this elegant emporium takes the shopping experience to the next level. Its spacious fit out allows for the entire range to be on display, and the browsing experience is quiet and almost reverent; as if I'm thumbing through clothes in a museum. Believe me, it's virtually impossible to walk out empty handed.

CUMULUS INC.

Modern Australian joint

45 Flinders Lane (near Throssell Lane) / +61 3 9650 1445
cumulusinc.com.au / Open daily

Andrew McConnell's Cumulus Inc. is always an absolute delight. Each time I return, it never fails to deliver remarkably good food, especially during lunch and dinner. I can vouch that the whole roast lamb shoulder is falling-off-the-bone tender — order it with iceberg lettuce for sweet relief. If you prefer smaller bites and a more casual dining experience, head upstairs and order the duck waffle and foie gras for its inventive burst of flavor. With industrial-chic furnishings, black steel windows and a cascading light feature, this stylish eatery draws boisterous crowds, bumps fab tunes and is always buzzing, no matter the time of day.

HIGHER GROUND

Aesthetically pleasing all-day dining

650 Little Bourke Street (at Spencer Street) / +61 3 8899 6219
highergroundmelbourne.com.au / Open daily

I admit, I'm constantly drawn to gorgeous eateries. Housed in a former power station, Higher Ground has 15-meter (50-foot) high ceilings, glorious arched windows and a cavernous space with a mezzanine level. There are bar seats for lone wanderers looking for a place to work, long tables for large groups and couches for chilling out. Open for breakfast, lunch and dinner, the ambiance varies and so does the food. During the day, I love digging in to their fragrant semolina porridge served with roasted and fresh blueberries, tonka beans and lemon balm. At night, the cured kingfish with ponzu, though small in portion, is refreshingly tart.

INCU STORE

Cosmopolitan wardrobe staples

Shop ACL12, QV Building, Albert Coates Lane (near Shilling Lane)
+61 3 9654 4725 / incu.com / Open daily

This upmarket, multi-label store started by brothers Brian and Vincent Wu is a curated assemblage of clothes, shoes and accessories from the trendiest American and European designers on the market. I personally feel the men's selection is stronger than the women's, and sometimes try on the more unisex-looking stuff in the hope that it fits me. Carrying brands like Rag & Bone, Etoile Isabel Marant, Kenzo and Karen Walker for the ladies, and A.P.C., Comme des Garcons, Saturdays NYC and their own label, Weathered, for gents, the overall style is effortlessly cool and made up of versatile pieces. The myriad colors and sheer variety make shopping here a thrill. If not for life's budget constraints, I would buy my entire wardrobe in this one store.

LUCY FOLK

Food-themed jewelry

1A Crossley Street (near Bourke Street) / +61 3 9663 6829
lucyfolk.com / Closed Sundau

Not to toot my own sartorial horn, but I've had many strangers compliment my pearl-adorned slap bracelet, taco friendship band and gold rice ring. I always dread when they ask me where they're from because my response is, "It's from Lucy Folk," and this spot is a secret I want to hoard for myself. This tiny boutique is one of those blink-and-you'll-miss-it types — unless you recognize the signature pretzel logo at the entrance. The Melbourne-based designer themes her jewelry around food, and when she started out, she actually electroplated real corn chips and popcorn. These days, she and her team use processes like lost wax casting and CAD rendering, as well as traditional gold and silversmithing. Her collections are quirky and delicate, yet timeless — exactly how I like it.

MAMASITA

A delicious slice of Mexico

1/11 Collins Street (near Collins Place) / +61 3 9650 3821
mamasita.com.au / Open daily

Once you're through the long line at Mamasita, you're guaranteed a meal that will knock your socks off. This fun, colorful taqueria is practically an institution, serving up fresh mouthfuls of crunchy tostaditas, moreish tacos and drool-worthy Mexican street corn: grilled corn on the cob doused in chipotle mayo, melty queso and tart lime. The fish taco, made with the local market's catch of the day, is my choice as it packs a punch with tangy red onion salsa, kicky achiote and crunchy cabbage. Wash it all down with a couple of classic margaritas and happy tunes.

METROPOLIS BOOKSHOP

Surprising reads and whimsical gifts

Level 3, Curtin House, 252 Swanston Street (near Lonsdale Street)
+61 3 9663 2015 / metropolisbookshop.com.au / Open daily

Browsing in Metropolis Bookshop is like walking around a vibrant square in the sky. Located on the third floor of Curtin House, slip into the elevator – or puff your way up the winding staircase – and immediately feel the hustle and bustle of the city melt away. To me, it's a wonderful place to de-stress. This indie bookstore specializes in premium graphic design, architecture, photography, culture and fashion titles, as well as a curated stock of non-fiction, fiction and children's books. I love thumbing through the hardcovers, and I never leave without picking up a witty greeting card.

ROOFTOP CINEMA

Movie night under the stars

Level 6, Curtin House, 252 Swanston Street (near Lonsdale Street)
+61 3 9654 5394 / rooftopcinema.com.au / Open December through April

What's better than movies in a dark cinema accompanied by ice cream cones? Movies on a rooftop with a glittering view of Melbourne CBD. When the weather gets beautifully balmy, I can't think of anything better to do on summer nights than head up to Rooftop Cinema. Showing a selection of arthouse, classic and recently released films, grab your tickets and a cocktail, and lounge in one of their comfortable Ici Et La deck chairs before the movie begins. It's a great place for a first date or hundredth date — just don't forget to bring a jacket (this is Melbourne, after all) or rent one of their blankets before the show.

ROYAL STACKS

Melbourne's reigning burger joint

470 Collins Street (near William Street) / +61 3 9620 0296
royalstacks.com.au / Open daily

If you, like me, think a good burger is one of God's gifts to mankind, look out for the neon pink burger sign on Collins Street. Royal Stacks pays homage to New York's infamous Shake Shack with its oozy beef burgers, scrumptious frozen custards and concrete mixers in flavors like New York cheesecake and a riff on Kinder Bueno. The single and double stacks are for those who like it uncomplicated, but if you're a bit more adventurous, go for Prince Harry or The King, which come with double cheddar and a mac and cheese croquette, respectively. Life can't get any better than that, right?

SHORTSTOP COFFEE & DONUTS

Fancy doughnuts

12 Sutherland Street (near Little Lonsdale Street) / No phone
short-stop.com.au / Open daily

"We start making our doughnuts at 4:30am daily," said Sinye Ooi, co-founder of Shortstop Coffee & Donuts. This hole-in-the-wall venue buzzes with life from the second their doors open, with everyone from men in suits to teenage girls striding in for their dose of fresh confections and coffee. Their maple walnut & brown butter raised treat is a dream that I could happily partake of every day, as it's chewy, crunchy and sweet all at once. When I crave floral flavors, I opt for the Earl Grey & rose cake variety, filled with lemon myrtle gel and dipped in a rose water and rose petal glaze. Once I've washed it down with their strong and refreshing New Orleans iced coffee made with vanilla bean and agave, I'm ready to face the world.

SPRING STREET GROCER

High-end supermarket

157 Spring Street (at Turnbull Alley) / +61 3 9639 0335
springstreetgrocer.com.au / Open daily

This gourmet grocery store reminds me of those provision shops in Europe, where you can spend hours absorbed in quality products you've never seen before. Spring Street Grocer supplies fresh, organic, wholesome and nutritious produce and pantry items that are handpicked. There's even a cute little cheese cellar in their basement where you can taste and smell some of the finest bries, camemberts and goudas available in Australia. I enjoy wandering in here before a party to pick up fromage or exotic sauces, and usually walk out with an extra treat – a sneaky scoop of pistachio from their amazing gelato bar.

TIPO 00

Intimate Italian

361 Little Bourke Street (near Rankins Lane) / +61 3 9942 3946
tipo00.com.au / Closed Sunday

When it comes to noodles, I'm most particular about the texture being smooth and al dente. Tipo 00 never disappoints — named after the freshly ground flour used to make pizza and pasta, their in-house renditions of tagliatelle and pappardelle are flawlessly silken. Your culinary journey starts off with their warm, homemade rosemary focaccia served with a generous dollop of ricotta. Go for the squid ink tagliolini topped with squid and bottarga or the braised Wagyu Scotch pappardelle. Both plates deliver surprisingly robust flavors that have found their way into my heart. Finish off with the "tipomisu," a dense brownie hollowed out and filled with mascarpone, cream, egg yolk, dark rum and sugar.

south melbourne

albert park, southbank

On a peerless blue-sky day, the southern suburbs of
Southbank and South Melbourne are unabashedly pretty.
Surrounded by picturesque rivers and lakes, this upscale
neighborhood attracts picnicking families, large groups
of friends and couples wanting a bit of a break from the
CBD. The options are diverse and limitless – I love hitting
up the charming South Melbourne Market (see pg 62)
for food, fresh fruit and flowers. Historically known as
Emerald Hill, South Melbourne is one of the city's oldest
suburban areas, known for its well-preserved Victorian-Era
streetscapes which are now home to a string of cafés and
craft shops. The sprawling South Melbourne extends into
glitzy Southbank, home to the famed Crown Casino and
its waterfront fine-dining options. With some of Australia's
most sophisticated galleries, museums and theaters all
concentrated in one area, this arty precinct is set to thrill
and whet your cultural appetite.

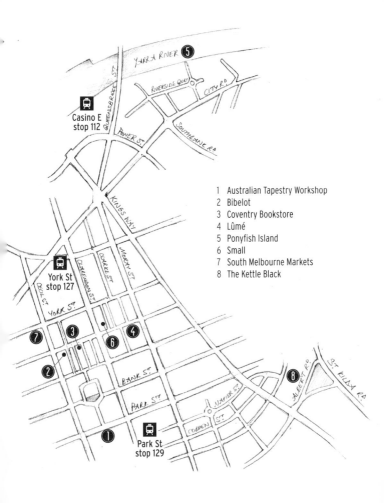

1 Australian Tapestry Workshop
2 Bibelot
3 Coventry Bookstore
4 Lûmé
5 Ponyfish Island
6 Small
7 South Melbourne Markets
8 The Kettle Black

AUSTRALIAN TAPESTRY WORKSHOP

The best of textile art

262–266 Park Street (near Perrins Street) / +61 3 9699 7885
austapestry.com.au / Open Tuesday through Friday

Occupying an almost fictitious-looking Victorian building — complete with a tower, decorative iron work and hooded bay windows — the Australian Tapestry Workshop is a unique institution dedicated to contemporary, hand-woven works that are created in collaboration with leading artists, architects and designers. Established in 1976, it's the only workshop of its kind in Australia and only one of a few around the globe. Its changing exhibitions are enjoyable and inspirational, and whenever I find time to visit, I leave energized. What's more, they also run public lectures, weaving classes, tours and an artist-in-residence program, so there's definitely something for everyone.

BIBELOT

Divine gelato and desserts

285-287 Coventry Street (near Hotham Street) / +61 3 9690 2688
bibelot.com.au / Open daily

There is gelato, and then there's gelato on a molten chocolate cone.
At Bibelot, there are two chocolate fountains — one dark and one milk —
which you can infuse your crunchy cones with. It's almost like there's a
second dessert party waiting to happen in your mouth when you're done
with the gelato. This patisserie and high tea salon also serves a lovely
selection of petits gâteaux, bonbons, macarons and delicate biscuits,
which you can take away or have in-house on their plush, Art Deco-style
cushions. Time to round up the squad and your reliable sweet tooth.

COVENTRY BOOKSTORE

Nostalgic nook for bookworms

265 Coventry Street (near Union Street) / +61 3 9686 8200
coventrybookstore.com.au / Open daily

If ever there was a bookshop that made me feel right at home, this is it.
The team at Coventry Bookstore takes on the spirit of a small, independent
boutique and they're wonderfully effervescent, encouraging slow browsing
in their timeless space. There are shelves of paperbacks and hardcovers
spanning all genres, from food and wine to interior design to philosophy.
There's an old-book smell that reminds me of my childhood, and a relaxing
jazz soundtrack that I usually find myself humming along to. I could easily
spend a day in here without even realizing where the time has gone.

LÛMÉ

Experimental dining

226 Coventry Street (near Craine Street) / +61 3 9690 0185
restaurantlume.com / Closed Sunday and Monday

If you have three hours to spare and want a spectacular dining experience, this is where you need to book. Lûmé is the brainchild of owner-chefs Shaun Quade and John-Paul Fiechtner, who have an amazing combined CV (Bo Innovation in Hong Kong and Le Chateaubriand in Paris are highlights). The fare here is truly inspired – there's an elegant quince and duck liver dish that makes you do a double take when you look closer. The dehydrated piece of quince arrives looking like duck liver, and the liver comes in the form of a parfait that could, from a distance, pass off as quince. Textures and flavors here are spot on, so come curious and ready to be sublimely surprised.

PONYFISH ISLAND

Boathouse pub vibes

Southbank Pedestrian Bridge (near Southbank Promenade)
No phone / ponyfish.com.au / Open daily

The name Ponyfish Island is already emblematic of what you're going to experience here. Situated under the Southbank Pedestrian Bridge on the Yarra River, this laid-back bar is literally its own island on the water and is the ultimate locale for kicking back with cold beers (I recommend whatever is on offer from Mountain Goat or Cricketers Arms) after work. It feels like you're in your own wooden boathouse, with colorful festoon lights hanging over the bar and chilled-out indie tunes to set the mood. Grab one of the bar stools overlooking Southbank or the CBD and a side of nachos or toasties for the win.

SMALLS

Teeny watering hole with stellar vino

20-22 Yarra Place (near Coventry Street) / +61 3 9686 2990
smallsbar.com.au / Closed Tuesday and Wednesday

With only 24 seats and a no-reservations policy, Smalls is exactly what
it sounds like, but with a worldly, sophisticated outlook. I love making
these digs part of my evening, especially when it's nice and quiet at 5pm.
The space is well thought-out – it blends both laneway and boutique lounge
atomspheres with its white-painted brick walls, herringbone parquet and
steel grid frames. It focuses on small wine producers from across the globe,
with an impressive wine list put together by sommelier Wiremu Andrews.
Their Hunter Valley sémillon and Abruzzo rosé are my drinks of choice.

SOUTH MELBOURNE MARKET

Local delights

Corner of Cecil and Coventry Streets / +61 3 9209 6295
southmelbournemarket.com.au / Open Wednesday and Friday
through Sunday

What I love most about the South Melbourne Market is how it caters mainly to locals and the community around it – the ambiance here is almost akin to a village where everyone has their own routine. On weekends, I visit the market for my dose of fresh produce and sweet blooms. Wander through the dim alleys and allow yourself to be captivated by the sights and aromas. Hungry? You'll have to join the line at Koy's gözleme hut or for Claypots Evening Star's grilled fish on bread, because these two are mouthwatering treats not to be missed.

THE KETTLE BLACK

Beautiful food and interiors

50 Albert Road (near Princes Highway) / +61 3 9088 0721
thekettleblack.com.au / Open daily

On any given day, The Kettle Black is where the action is and you'll see why pretty quickly. There's a handsome marble fireplace and countertop, hanging plants, hexagonal tiles and tinges of gold on the shelves and walls. Light streams in from its floor-to-ceiling windows and fills the stylish space with a luminous glow. You'll likely be wondering the same thing I always do: "How do I make my home look like this?" Coffees are from Market Lane, 5 Senses and Small Batch, so you're guaranteed a good cuppa. Food here is slightly more upmarket than the usual brunch fare – expect dishes like chili scrambled eggs with house cured kangaroo, polenta porridge with burnt maple and a gorgeous fresh snapper on a brioche roll. Believe me, you'll be telling all your friends about it.

GLEADELL STREET MARKET

Market Trawl

Local produce, vintage wear and trendy food stalls

CAMBERWELL SUNDAY MARKET
Market Place (near Prospect Hill Road; Camberwell)
no phone, camberwellsundaymarket.org
open Sunday

GLEADELL STREET MARKET
Gleadell Street (near Bridge Road; Richmond)
+61 3 9205 5555, yarracity.vic.gov.au/Events/Shopping-
and-dining/markets/Gleadell-Street, open Saturday

LOST AND FOUND MARKET
511 Lygon Street (near Albion Street; Brunswick East)
+61 3 9383 1883, lostandfoundmarket.com.au
open Saturday and Sunday

NIGHT NOODLE MARKET
Birrarung Marr Park, Batman Avenue (near Flinders
Lane; CBD), no phone, goodfoodmonth.com.au/
melbourne, Open two weeks in November annually

QUEEN VICTORIA MARKET
Corner of Queen and Therry Streets (CBD)
+61 3 9320 5822, thenightmarket.com.au
Wednesday nights, November through March

NIGHT NOODLE MARKET

There's nothing more satisfying than going to one of Melbourne's many weekend or seasonal markets on a gloriously sunny day. Whether it's picking up fresh fruit, digging through piles for terrific secondhand finds or looking for a perch to enjoy live music, I find that markets appeal to just about everybody – and they don't discriminate either.

The **Camberwell Sunday Market** is the prime place to rummage through pre-loved clothes, crafts and bric-a-brac that could put a real spin on your outfit or home décor. Operating since 1976, this vibrant, open-air market is the city's biggest for gently used items with about 370 outdoor stalls every weekend.

On Saturdays, layer on the sunscreen and bring an empty trolley bag to the **Gleadell Street Market**, a buzzing fresh food emporium overflowing with fruits and vegetables, warm bread, herbs, flowers and other gourmet pleasures. I normally come ready to chat to stall owners and sample a bunch of different things.

Meanwhile, if you're over at Brunswick East on the weekend, pop over to **Lost & Found Market**, a melting pot of old-school furniture, lighting, art, books and records. This shopping paradise has over 60 retro-looking stalls and an excellent team of staff ready to help the minute you ask. It's also an ideal place to people-watch as bearded hipsters and creative types traipse in hoards.

Once summer hits, I'm often at the **Noodle Night Market**, which is on for two weeks every November. It's a 10-minute walk from my home and hosts a multitude of trendy eateries such as Messina, Mr. Miyagi (see pg 95) and Wonderbao. My ideal scenario happens on a grassy hill, seaweed taco in one hand and a glass of wine in the other. This market attracts a suitably cool (and large) crowd, so come prepared for queues.

Queen Victoria Market hosts a yearly summer and winter night market for a little over three months at a time, gathering some of Melbourne's hottest food stalls, artisans and performers under one roof. It's a fantastic place to gather with friends and share an array of treats – my picks are Simply Spanish's paella and Running Man's icy sangria.

richmond

cremorne

—◆—

On the surface, Richmond looks a bit, well, unappealing. Many know it for being near to sporting hub East Melbourne, where the Australian Open and Australian Football League (AFL) matches are held, and for Little Saigon, an eclectic strip on Victoria Street littered with Asian grocers and the most scrumptious Vietnamese food in town. Others would be acquainted with the outlet shopping on Bridge Road or the pub grub on Swan Street. A scant three kilometers southeast of the CBD, Richmond has been the subject of gentrification since the early 1990s and its diversity makes it an interesting option for anyone looking to explore somewhere more local. I personally enjoy the quirks and unpredictability of the area – amidst the attractions on Bridge Road and Swan Street is a plethora of great cafés, charming shops and fine dining hideouts. Lying just south of Richmond is Cremorne, an industrial area with many fashion and design offices as well as hole-in-the-wall coffeeshops.

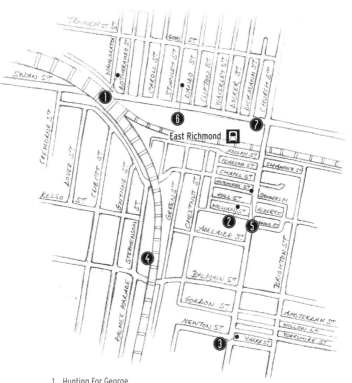

East Richmond

1   Hunting For George
2   Jardan
3   Kong BBQ
4   Little Company
5   Pana Chocolate
6   The Meatball & Wine Bar
7   The Ugly Duckling Wine &
    Cocktail Bar

HUNTING FOR GEORGE

Housewares emporium

31 Wangaratta Street (near Tanner Street) / +61 3 9421 4849
huntingforgeorge.com / Open Friday and Saturday

Hunting For George takes homewares shopping to new levels with its broad range of bed linens, furniture, plant accessories and art prints. While their online emporium has an easy deliver-to-your-doorstep option, it's their showroom in Richmond that truly inspires. Head down and browse through their collection of local and international brands such as Armadillo & Co, Blacklist Studio, Pop & Scott and Ivy Muse Botanical Emporium (see pg 92) – and purchase right then and there if you please. Open every Friday and Saturday, the goodies from this stunning, well-curated space are ones you'll brag to all your friends about.

JARDAN

Luxurious, handcrafted furniture

522 Church Street (near Albert Street) /+61 3 8581 4988
jardan.com.au / Open daily

If I could have my home filled with goods from one store, it would be Jardan. The handmade furnishings are understated and incredibly stunning, plus the small, Australian-owned company has been awarded the country's highest environmental rating and accredited as a carbon-neutral organization. Stepping in here is like walking into your dream house. Filled with natural light and warm tones, the first floor showcases Jardan's Modernist-inspired sofas, tables and chairs, while the second story incorporates an open-plan kitchen, outdoor setting and entertainment area. Their Wilfred sofa – featuring an exposed solid American oak frame with plush cushioning made from feathers and down – is on my wish list every single year. One of these days...

KONG BBQ

Inventive, Asian-inspired plates

599 Church Street (near Yarra Street) / +61 3 9427 1307
kongbbq.com.au / Open daily

Using age-old barbeque and smoking techniques, Kong BBQ brings delectable
Korean fried wings, baby back pork ribs, beef strip loin and an assortment
of pillowy steamed buns to the table. It's a hip, boisterous joint with warm
camaraderie that makes for the ideal start to any weekend. The team spent
an entire year perfecting the menu before opening, and that thoughtful time
and careful consideration is obvious in their food — the pork belly and soft
shell crab baos, wood-roasted salmon and fried rice with kimchi and beef
brisket are items not to be missed. Grab your A Team and share everything.

LITTLE COMPANY

Flawless facials

79 Stephenson Street (near Balmain Street) / +61 3 9421 1293
littlecompany.com.au / Closed Sunday

As far as beauty secrets go, this place is my biggest one. Hidden down
a blink-and-you'll-miss-it laneway nestled between eateries and design
companies, the entrance to this haven is discreet, marked only by a sign
on top of their converted warehouse space. It's a beautiful spa once you
enter – there's lush foliage everywhere alongside exposed white-washed
brick walls, gold-and-black light fixtures and a spacious hallway that leads
to your very own cocoon. Employing firm massage methods and natural
products from Sodashi and MV Skincare, their facials cater specifically to
your skin type, smell like a tropical island and deliver a brilliant glow that
lasts for days.

PANA CHOCOLATE

Raw chocolate bar

491 Church Street (near Albert Street)
+61 3 0071 7488 / panachocolate.com
Open daily

I'd always been cynical about how delicious "healthy chocolate" could taste – that is until I came across Pana Chocolate. Founded by Pana Barbounis, the cocoa here is smooth, rich and infused with antioxidants, amino acids, vitamins and minerals. What's more, these treats don't contain any preservatives and are vegan, gluten-free, dairy-free and soy-free. While you can get the bars (coconut & goji is the way to go) at specialty supermarkets, you'll have to visit their shop in Richmond for their tasty raw cake slices, which come in flavors like blueberry and lemon, and caramel chocolate chunk. The best part? They taste better than a cake packed with sugar and butter. Really!

THE MEATBALL & WINE BAR

A carnivore's dream

105 Swan Street (near Stanley Street) / +61 3 9428 3339
meatballandwinebar.com.au / Open daily

Who doesn't love a good meatball? These round,mounds of meat take me
to my happy place. Toss that in with al dente pasta and you'll have a match
made in heaven. The Meatball & Wine Bar is a dimly lit, intimate noshery with
an extensive menu centered around hearty balls of pork, beef, chicken, fish or
a veggie mixture of quinoa, corn and cheese served with your choice of sauce
(tomato, cream or pesto salsa verde) and base – cannellini beans, creamy
polenta, mashed potatoes, house pasta or a market vegetable. Their silky and
soft burrata or premium beef carpaccio also makes for an excellent starter.
Two words: dig in.

THE UGLY DUCKLING WINE & COCKTAIL BAR

Imbibe in an indoor garden

238 Swan Street (near Church Street) / **+61 3 9429 1498**
theuglyduckling.com.au / **Open daily**

With impressive high ceilings, blonde wood furnishings and sunshine streaming in from the skylight roof in the atrium, this sleek bar looks like a stylish beer garden. The mood is relaxing, as if you're having a tipple in someone's home, and the crowd is mainly local. Choose from an extensive list of classic beverages like a Tom Collins or Singapore Sling, or a creative number such as the Corpse Reviver #86, which blends Tanqueray, Jameson and La Quintinye Blanc with blood orange shrub, lemon juice and a dash of absinthe for a strong and complex yet refreshing taste.

camberwell

hawthorn

Convivial, spiffy and somewhat yuppie, the eastern
suburbs of Hawthorn and Camberwell – the last bastions of
post-Gold Rush wealth – are frequented by families and
university students. I love the spirit about these areas:
they're manicured enough to look pretty in pictures,
but are without the stuffiness that comes with most upscale
districts. There's been a massive dining revival here,
so head over and grab a bite at one of the many cafés and
nosheries that have recently opened their doors along the
effervescent Glenferrie Road. With lots of open space and
cheerful shopfront windows, Burke Road in Camberwell
makes for a fun shopping experience. Spend some time
hanging out in this self-contained neighborhood and you'll
find it difficult to leave.

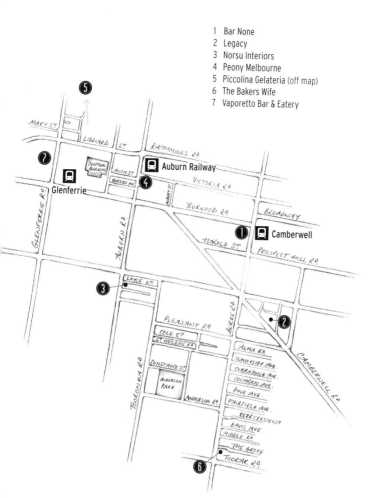

1 Bar None
2 Legacy
3 Norsu Interiors
4 Peony Melbourne
5 Piccolina Gelateria (off map)
6 The Bakers Wife
7 Vaporetto Bar & Eatery

BAR NONE

Local cocktail lounge

72 Auburn Parade (near Burke Road) +61 3 9882 1086
barnone.com.au / Closed Sunday and Monday

There's no better drinking hole in Camberwell than Bar None. Tucked down a laneway next to a train station, this obscure, underground bar offers some of the most creative concoctions I've ever seen. Sweet jazz and old-school rock tunes fill the Art Deco space strewn with plush couches and tables, and I can't think of another bar that feels more comfortable or homey than this. Feeling peckish? Order the pastrami-laden Reuben or dips and Turkish bread as the ideal accompaniment to your beverage of choice.

LEGACY

Where healthy and hearty flavors collide

347 Camberwell Road (near Avenue Road) / +61 3 9041 1796
facebook.com/Legacycamberwell / Open daily

This brekkie has a truly humongous menu – it'll knock your socks off and have you coming back so that you can try more. From superfood porridge to passionfruit panna cotta to buttermilk fried chicken, there's definitely something for all taste buds. Or if you, like me, want the best of both worlds, go for the genius breakfast board, which gives you a fresh orange juice and a mini açaí bowl, a croissant and a smashed avocado with egg on toast. Its red brick-and-timber minimalist interior is stylish yet undeniably homey, and is an unparalleled landscape for your casual afternoon hangouts.

NORSU INTERIORS

Nordic-chic furnishings

303 Auburn Road (near Broomfield Road) / +61 3 9882 5887
norsu.com.au / Closed Sunday

Norsu Interiors will always have a special place in my heart. When I moved to Melbourne and was looking to furnish my new home, this was one of the first places I chanced upon. A pioneer in bringing Scandinavian stylings to town, their eye for detail is spot on, and their curation of housewares is impeccable. With a strong Nordic design sensibility, Nat Wheeler and Kristy Sadlier's choice of products fill a hole in the Australian market – soft furnishings in blush and gray, fun artwork and elegant knick-knacks in gold, copper and black steel. I bought a handsome copper ladder and a cowhide rug – two years later, I have absolutely no regrets about either of them.

PEONY MELBOURNE

A touch of luxe

107 Auburn Road (near Newburgh Place) / +61 3 9882 0662
peonymelbourne.com.au / Closed Sunday and Monday

The chic Jill Timms, owner of Peony Melbourne, is the sort of woman who knows her regulars by name and insists on writing every sales receipt by hand. "I run a very personalized shopping experience," she said. Her haute parfumerie is an absolute dream and reminds me of the amazing gems you stumble upon in suburban Paris. Upon arriving, a cocoon of fragrances envelops you and you're not sure where to start looking – there's shelves of elegant perfume bottles, gorgeous candles and dainty beauty products of little known (at least, in Australia) brands. Jill gets most of her upmarket haul from Milan and Florence, and only stocks labels that aren't available anywhere else in Melbourne. Some examples include the esteemed By Kilian, Amouage, Cire Trudon and Santa Maria Novella.

PICCOLINA GELATERIA

Traditional Southern Italian-style gelato

802 Glenferrie Road (near Measham Place) / +61 3 9815 2815
facebook.com/pg/piccolinagelateria / Open daily

When Sandra Foti realized that she couldn't buy anything similar to her father's creamy, all-natural, homemade gelato, she decided to open Piccolina Gelateria. Armed with secret family recipes, Sandra went to Italy to hone her skills in preparation for her new venture. There are now more than 20 gelato, sorbetti and granita flavors here, but my personal poisons are the pistachio and the chocolate brownie. This cozy yet contemporary space has people spilling out the doors on weekends, so grab your army and lap up the experience.

THE BAKERS WIFE

Pleasant brunch and baked goods

414 Burke Road (near The Grove) / +61 3 9809 1133
thebakerswife.com.au / Open daily

Whether you call it a bakery or café, you can't deny that The Bakers Wife ticks all the right boxes. Decked out with impressively high ceilings and an industrial aesthetic, it cleverly demarcates the sections in its large space to make it feel more homey. There's communal seating, bar seating, couches and a courtyard for when the weather is fine. Try their crushed avocado on multigrain toast, which is plated up with crisp quinoa and a poached egg, creating a sumptuous blend of textures and flavors. Pair that with a latte or flat white, served sweet and bold with a hint of red berries and cocoa.

VAPORETTO BAR & EATERY

Venetian cuisine and wine bar

681 Glenferrie Road (near Grace Street) / +61 3 9078 5492
vaporetto.com.au / Open daily

There are few things that bring me more joy than dining with a bunch of friends in Vaporetto's sunny courtyard on a marvelous spring day with a Negroni in hand (yes, they do a mean Negroni). It's Melbourne meets Venice, with a relaxed vibe and cheery elegance in its colorful walls. Try their squid ink tagliatelle with tiger prawns and lobster sauce; I daresay it'll be one of the freshest recipes you'll ever taste. The pasta is perfectly al dente, and the prawns taste like they went directly from sea to pot. Otherwise, the slow-cooked pork in milk, sage, fennel seed and lemon thyme is a pretty tempting option, too.

delectable asian fusion fare

Best of both worlds

CHIN CHIN
125 Flinders Lane (near Higson Lane; CBD)
+61 3 8663 2000, chinchinrestaurant.com.au, open daily

CODA
Basement, 141 Flinders Lane (near Oliver Lane; CBD)
+61 3 9650 3155, codarestaurant.com.au, open daily

MAGIC MOUNTAIN SALOON
62 Little Collins Street (near Exhibition Street; CBD)
+61 3 9078 0078, magicmountainsaloon.com.au
open daily

RICE PAPER SCISSORS
19 Liverpool Street (near Little Bourke Street; CBD)
+61 3 9663 9890, ricepaperscissors.com.au, open daily

SUPERNORMAL
180 Flinders Lane (near Watson Place; CBD)
+61 3 9650 8688, supernormal.net.au, open daily

Like the influx of varied cultures that now populate Melbourne, some of this city's top-notch gastronomic experiences are a beautiful blend of cuisines that mix Australian produce with Asian ingredients and techniques. Expect robust dishes with a complex layering of flavors, rich aromas and incredible fare full of heart – which is ultimately what dining in this food-centric city is all about.

There is often a long wait, but that doesn't deter anyone from joining the **Chin Chin** bandwagon, which has everyone falling for their refreshing kingfish sashimi and the satisfying caramelized sticky pork served with chili vinegar and a sour herb salad. Can't decide? Go for the chef's choice "Feed Me" menu, a feast for the entire table.

Neon-lit **Magic Mountain Saloon** is a fun, relaxed morning-to-late-night concept that combines Thai and Australian flavors. The breakfast menu is all about comfort food; think coconut and lime chicken noodle soup and toasted crumpets with sweet pandan. Lunches and dinners are more inventive – try the hot-and-sour baby snapper, king prawn salad with green apple, and lemongrass and curried soft shell crab.

It may not look like much from the outside, but step into this basement restaurant and let your senses be overwhelmed. **Coda** serves up refined, Vietnamese-influenced fare. My must-haves are the aromatic roasted yellow duck curry and succulent Crystal Bay prawns with chili jam.

Supernormal is a stunningly executed space with plates influenced by Tokyo, Shanghai, Hong Kong and Seoul. The cavernous dining room incorporates playful features such as a Japanese vending machine and a basement karaoke room. An entrée that ticks all the right boxes is the pan-roasted John Dory with burnt butter, wild watercress and shaved kombu.

Rice Paper Scissors is fashioned after Southeast Asia's hawker centers. There's a convivial ambiance and rich, flavorful plates designed to share. Kick off dinner with a delicious Asian-inspired cocktails, like the Thai Sangria (pineapple, mango, Thai herbs and white wine). The sticky pork belly drizzled in tamarind caramel sauce and chargrilled Wagyu beef are heaven on a plate.

prahran

armadale, windsor

It's not surprising to see ultra-stylish folks strutting around the enclaves of Prahran, Windsor and Armadale. Originally settled by European settlers in the 1830s, it became popular with wealthy citizens, and its upper-class reputation has continued through to today as these inner southeast areas attract a supremely posh crowd. The heart of the hoods is Chapel Street, a glitzy strip known for everything from its upscale fashion labels to the hippest restaurants and cafés. I actually prefer shopping here over the CBD for the very fact that everything is located down this one (extremely) long street, and I don't have to run around looking for a particular store like a headless chook. That said, Greville Street is home to tons of places to gander, like an old-school, British-style barber, French bistros and record stores. Call your trusty shopping troop, because you'll need them – along with an interest-free credit card.

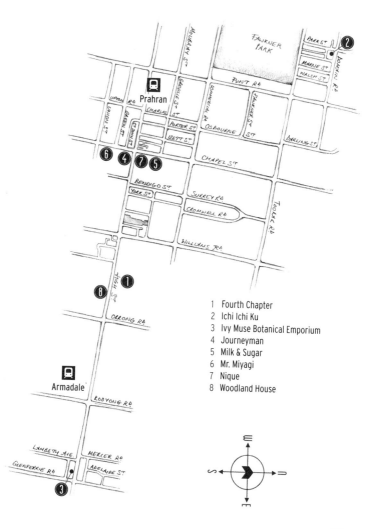

1 Fourth Chapter
2 Ichi Ichi Ku
3 Ivy Muse Botanical Emporium
4 Journeyman
5 Milk & Sugar
6 Mr. Miyagi
7 Nique
8 Woodland House

FOURTH CHAPTER

Brunch in a bright, leafy setting

385 High Street (near Trinian Street) / +61 3 9510 2277
fourthchapter.com.au / Open daily

Beyond Fourth Chapter's stately white door is a brilliant menu that balances healthy options with cheeky indulgences. I'm not much of a health nut, but I find myself craving their power-packed açaí bowl at least once a week and do whatever it takes to get it. Chock-full of sweet berries, granola and three splendid dollops of peanut butter, this lip-smacking combination is full of great textures and makes for a satisfyingly full meal. Also on offer is a beetroot and cheddar waffle, smashed avocado with corn tempura and smoky popcorn, and a slew of nutritious drinks such as smoothies, kombucha and a turmeric latte.

ICHI ICHI KU

Hole-in-the-wall Japanese food

119 Park Street (near Domain Road) / +61 3 9820 9119
ichiichiku.com.au / Open daily

Take note, sushi fans. This tiny izakaya looks like it belongs in an alleyway in Kyoto and delivers bold, fresh flavors in the form of their glistening rolls. I'm obsessed with the Ichi Ni Roll – brown sushi rice wrapped with lobster, avocado and cucumber then topped with seared salmon belly and mayonnaise. The ingredients are top-notch and pair well together, with the juicy lobster balancing nicely against the lightly salted salmon. This gem also does some of the best gyoza and udon in town. If you don't feel like leaving your room, you're in luck: they deliver.

IVY MUSE BOTANICAL EMPORIUM

Sleek flora accessories

1250 High Street (near Glenferrie Road) / +61 3 9939 0228
ivymuse.com.au / Open daily

The brainchild of longtime friends Jacqui Vidal and Alana Langan, this purveyor sells exquisite indoor garden accessories, like geometric plant stands, simple pots and minimalist planters. Their bright store is an aesthete's dream, with white walls and 24-carat gold-plated shelves that emphasize the unbridled beauty of its lush greenery. They also stock gorgeous copper watering cans and classy marble trays that will enliven any home (or Pinterest account). Being in here always calms me and makes me wish I could turn my home into a manicured jungle.

JOURNEYMAN

Hearty fare in an industrial-chic eatery

169 Chapel Street (near St John Street) / +61 3 9521 4884
journeymancafe.com.au / Open daily

Journeyman is ideal for a respite from shopping. The sophisticated fit out showcases exposed brick, timber paneling and a welcoming communal table. When it comes to food, the talented team has it down pat. They do one of the tastiest Bircher mueslis around, as it's made to exactly the right consistency and whipped with fresh, seasonal fruit and organic yogurt. Otherwise, their smashed avocado with hummus and candied bacon is pure creative genius and a local favorite. Time only for a coffee? The baristas make a mean single-origin espresso, with aromatic flavors that will have you coming back for more.

MILK & SUGAR

Wallet-friendly designer décor

207 Chapel Street (near High Street) / +61 3 9521 7074
milkandsugar.com.au / Open daily

I adore everything about this home goods store, from the pastel hues of its plates and bowls to the printed cushions to the summery vibes of the artwork hanging on the walls. Being in here makes me feel like I'm in the middle of LA's stylish Abbot Kinney Boulevard with the beach steps away. Take it from me, if you're looking to redecorate your home on a budget, Milk & Sugar will meet all your needs. Even if you're not trying to do a complete redesign, you'll still walk out with a gold-flecked teacup, like I did. Resistance is futile here.

MR. MIYAGI

Japanese fusion eats

99 Chapel Street (near Union Street) / +61 3 9529 5999
mrmiyagi.com.au / Closed Monday

RECOMMENDED BY
TRAVIS SANDERS
OWNER AND FOUNDER OF FARMGATE CHEESE

I would sum up my experience at Mr. Miyagi (and repeat encounters) in one word: divine. A major part of why this modern Japanese restaurant is so beloved is its salmon nori taco, composed of a blend of popping textures and flavors within its fried seaweed shell. There's grilled salmon belly, sushi rice, spicy cabbage, Japanese mayo and chili oil – what's not to love? Add to that a few pieces of Miyagi fried chicken, Wagyu beef tataki and a green tea soba noodle salad, and you'll be rolling home happy. Things to note: getting a table can take about an hour on a weekday and up to two hours on the weekend, but their cocktail bar at the back is definitely one to check out as you wait.

NIQUE

Black, grey and white threads

201 Chapel Street (near High Street) / +61 3 9525 2153
nique.com.au / Open daily

Much like the style of this independent label, Nique's flagship store delivers a clean and minimalistic shopping experience. Founders Nick and Lucy Ennis started out as a local design studio before further developing their aesthetic and catapulting into what is now a distinctly edgy brand with a loyal following. Its pieces for men and women are Scandinavian in style and crafted from unique materials such as bamboo cotton and soybean fabric. I'm a huge fan of their black dresses – seriously, us ladies can never have too many – as the shapes are relaxed and ideal for traipsing around the city.

WOODLAND HOUSE

A dressed-up affair

78 Williams Road (near High Street) / +61 3 9525 2178
woodlandhouse.com.au / Closed Monday

Fresh produce plays a huge part in Melbourne's fine-dining scene, and that's especially so at Woodland House. This degustation-focused establishment is led by Thomas Woods and Hayden McFarland, who both believe that an innovative, veggie-based cuisine is key. I, like many others, have left raving about the exceptional quality of their food. There's wood-roasted mussels with asparagus and salted egg yolk, a basic but cracking dish. Another must-try is the mind-blowingly tender grilled Wagyu served with oyster sauce, fermented shiitake and sesame; it had me salivating for days. Bring whoever you wish to impress – this is exactly the place for it.

MELBOURNE AFTER DARK:
classy cocktails

The city's top libations

BAR AMERICANO
20 Presgrave Place (near Little Collins Street; CBD)
no phone, baramericano.com, closed Sunday

BLACK PEARL
304 Brunswick Street (near Johnston Street; Fitzroy)
+61 3 9417 0455, blackpearlbar.com.au, open daily

EAU DE VIE
1 Malthouse Lane (near Flinders Lane; CBD)
+61 4 1282 5441, eaudevie.com.au, open daily

HIHOU
1 Flinders Lane (near Spring Street; CBD)
+61 3 9654 5465, hihou.com.au, closed Sunday

LUI BAR
Level 55, Rialto Towers, 525 Collins Street (near King
Street; CBD), +61 3 9691 3888, luibar.com.au, open daily

Melbourne certainly has no lack of a nightlife – with numerous bars, pubs and other niche watering holes peppered around the city and the inner suburbs, everyone has their local and earmarks for a night out. My preferred wind-down spaces are usually dim, stylish and hidden-away lounges that thrive on infusing their creativity into a glass.

Once you find the entrance to **Bar Americano** at the end of Presgrave Place (look for the blue Tabacchi sign), you're in for a real treat. This standing-room-only venue is an homage to the time of the "American Bar," when upper-class Europeans discovered liquid delights in Chicago and New York City. Sticking to their guns and serving only Prohibition-Era classics – with the exception of a Christmas concoction, usually made with port, rum or whisky, and garnished with delish spices like cinnamon, cloves and nutmeg – this is a flawless pint-sized joint for all occasions.

Looking for a spectacular view? You'll love **Lui Bar**, perched on the 55th floor of the striking Rialto Towers. The cavernous space is oh-so-chic and decked out with a breathtaking "chandelier" of transparent clouds, created with industrial residual plastic. My fancy drink of choice? The Gin-ger Spritz, a spicy and sweet libation that makes for a wonderful aperitif. Come dressed to the nines, because you'll be surrounded by a multitude of coiffed men and women enjoying a pre- or post-dinner concoction in this stunning venue.

For Old-World opulence, **Eau De Vie** is just the ticket. This hard-to-find speakeasy is located behind wooden, sign-free doors, but once you've made your entrance, expect boisterous jazz tunes and waist-coated staff to politely guide you to a table. Serving up some of the country's best whisky, lovers of single malts will be overjoyed by their extensive menu. Otherwise, their refreshing Yuzu Mule (vodka, yuzu curd, lime and house-made ginger beer) is not to be missed.

Black Pearl is a sophisticated drinking den filled with locals who enjoy a refined creation. With warm timbers and plush leather banquettes, it's ideal for groups of friends looking for a place to chill out, or for couples cozying up on a date. Try the Little Squirt, an appealing blend of tequila, yellow Chartreuse, lemon, mezcal, red capsicum and grapefruit soda.

Occupying the corner of Spring Street and Flinders Lane is an amazing sake den that will feed all your sake, whisky and Japanese snack cravings. **Hihou** is a sleek, minimalist bar with wooden blocks, concrete walls and a long, black marble group table. Their seasonal fruit libations are heavenly (if it's available, I highly recommend the kiwi) and you'll have to pair it with their Hihou dog, an arabiki pork sausage stuffed in a soft sesame brioche.

EAU DE VIE

MELBOURNE AFTER DARK:
all that jazz

From big bands to sultry soloists

BENNETTS LANE JAZZ CLUB
25 Bennetts Lane (near Little Lonsdale Street; CBD)
+61 3 9663 2856, bennettslane.com
check website for schedule

BIRD'S BASEMENT
11 Singers Lane (near William Street; CBD)
+61 1300 225 229, birdsbasement.com
open daily

PARIS CAT JAZZ CLUB
6 Goldie Place (near Little Bourke Street; CBD)
+61 4 1621 0979, pariscat.com.au
open Wednesday through Saturday

UPTOWN JAZZ CAFÉ
177 Brunswick Street (near King William Street;
Fitzroy), +61 3 9416 4546, uptownjazzcafe.com
open Wednesday through Saturday

Melburnians love jazz. Since the early 1920s, the brassy sound has been a popular form of entertainment in the city, and today, the jazz clubs are still packed out nightly by diverse groups looking for a good time. Nestled in the city's laneways (the obscure, underground factor makes them even more appealing), these live music joints are a worthwhile experience.

Though it's most renowned as a jazz bar, **Bennetts Lane Jazz Club** is committed to hosting local and international musicians spanning all genres. Its two iconic rooms have seen hundreds of gigs by such artists as Prince, Maceo Parker and Allan Browne. The staff here is remarkably hospitable, and the venue is an unpretentious place to have a bite, a beverage and be swept away by the soothing tunes.

Boasting a basement, a gallery and a loft, **Paris Cat Jazz Club** is housed in a three-story warehouse that offers a lively atmosphere that harkens back to France's post-war jazz scene. The iconic basement room has hosted incredible performers such as Don Burrows, The Melbourne Symphony Orchestra and even

Robbie Williams. If you're after tapas and libations with friends, pop up to the second level, which has a more laid-back mood.

Linked to the legendary Birdland, **Bird's Basement** is the well-known hot spot's first venture outside of New York City and delivers a similar experience in Melbourne – one where you can have solid tunes and an exceptional selection of food and drinks, without compromising on either. The modern 200-seat venue hosts myriad Australian soloists and funky jazz bands, and is committed to playing two dinner shows every evening.

Over in Fitzroy and craving some mellow grooves? No problem. **Uptown Jazz Café** sits above street level up an inconspicuous flight of stairs. This quirky place has played host to bop masters Charlie Parker, Bernie McGann and Miles Davis. Once you find your way in, prop yourself up by the bar with a tipple and an Asian fusion meal if you're peckish, and enjoy line-ups by a range of contemporary, up-and-coming musicians.

st kilda

It's no Bondi, but the beachside suburb of St Kilda has its own distinctive charm. The beaming face of the Luna Park gates are as iconic as the constant buzz from cafés and bars on the eclectic Acland and Fitzroy Streets. One of my very favorite ways to relax is to pop down to St Kilda Pier and slowly walk all the way to the edge of the water at sunset. You're hardly alone as there are always families and couples alike out this way, but the crashing waves are always calming and soul-soothing. Once a seedy hideout home to many prominent musicians, artists and subcultures, this bohemian neighborhood began its gentrification process 20 years ago. While a vibrant party scene and local music and film festival culture still exist, St Kilda now also appeals to young professionals and backpackers from all over the world. Go on, head down and see what the fuss is about.

1 Aurora Spa
2 Claypots Seafood Bar
3 I Carusi Ii
4 Milk the Cow

5 Scout House
6 Stokehouse
7 The Astor Theatre
8 Uncle

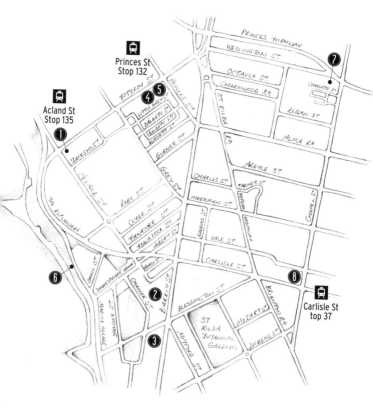

AURORA SPA

Top-notch face and body treatments

The Prince, 2 Acland Street (near Fitzroy Street) / +61 3 9536 1130
auroraspa.com.au / Open daily

Located at The Prince (see pg 9), this light-filled, two-story day spa is hands down my top pampering choice in Melbourne. Once you check in, you'll be guided to the relaxation lounge where you're given a consultation card and a warm cup of delicious herbal tea. Come early and take your time to soak in the view of the pristine bay and try out some of the amazing, plant-based ASPAR skin products available in the lounge. Their Unwind Retreat, including a signature kitya karnu (full-body exfoliation, hair treatment, facial mask and cool river stone ritual) in a private steam room and an hour-long massage, is my personal relaxation preference. Bliss out, folks.

CLAYPOTS SEAFOOD BAR

Seafood under the stars

213 Barkly Street (near Acland Street) / +61 3 9534 1282
facebook.com/claypotsstkilda / Open daily

This is where I want to celebrate my next birthday... and every birthday
following that. Claypots Seafood Bar is as dreamy as it is unpretentious,
serving up fresh, toothsome seafood that rivals the offerings anywhere in
Southeast Asia. Get your fix of mussels, oysters, grilled snapper, garlic king
prawns and their version of seafood stew, which is served up in clay pots.
On a balmy summer evening, sit out in the dimly-lit courtyard – where tiny
boats hang from trees – and bask in the unrivalled view of the stars and
faint scent of the sea. Otherwise, enjoy live music indoors and watch as the
chefs prepare your meal.

I CARUSI II

Pizza and pasta in a convivial space

231 Barkly Street (near Blessington Street) / +61 3 9593 6033
icarusiii.com.au / Open daily

Everything about I Carusi II is pitch-perfect, from the crispy, thin pie bases
to the white linen tablecloths. The beachside restaurant is warm and
energetic, and is the kind of place your parents would love – in a good way.
Bring an empty stomach because portions are generous. Start off with their
bruschetta and platter of calamari, prawns and fish, before moving on to
their 12-inch pizzas. I'm obsessed with the caprese (tomato, fiore di latte,
soppressa, basil fresh tomato), gamberi piccante (tomato, fiore di latte,
tiger prawns, chili, semi-dried tomatoes, basil) and No.26 (D.O.P. gorgonzola,
sautéed leeks and mozzarella), and have a very hard time choosing a top pick.
You'll leave feeling happy and satisfied, but without that rich, heavy feeling
in your stomach.

MILK THE COW

Cheese and wine party

157 Fitzroy Street (near Princes Street)   +61 3 9537 2225
milkthecow.com.au   Open daily

There are few things more quintessentially Australian than a feast of vino and fromage. Head over to Milk the Cow for a wide selection of delectable dairy and good, old-fashioned, country hospitality. Try their cheese and booze flights, which are brought out on wooden boards and showcase three to four options paired with boutique alcoholic choices, ranging from mainstays wine and beer to whisky, sake, bubbly and cognac. These draw out the flavors and it's a fun experience, whether it's your first time or fiftieth. If those aren't for you, their individual fondue pots served with warm crusty bread, are gooey and melt-in-your-mouth amazingness.

SCOUT HOUSE

Vintage curios meet designer homewares

161A Fitzroy Street (near Princes Street) / +61 3 9525 4343
scouthouse.com.au / Open daily

From decorative wooden crates to table settings to brass bed frames, Scout House has all your bases covered. Owner Orlando Mesiti traverses the globe to source quality products for his gem of a store. Striking a balance between throwback and modern, practical and quirky, I never know what to focus on when I step inside. Give me another 15 minutes and I'm nicely settled into browse mode, taking in everything from floor to ceiling. It feels like a European-influenced home that's chock-full of things I never knew I needed, and I usually leave with a small gift for myself — I've headed out of here toting a boar bristle hair brush, Cire Trudon candles and even a set of enamel cups and plates. Happy shopping!

STOKEHOUSE

Los Angeles-style beach house

30 Jacka Boulevard (near The Esplanade) / +61 3 9525 5555
stokehouse.com.au/Melbourne / Open daily

It's hard to miss this glorious building on the beach. Standing bright and tall with the crashing waves behind it, Stokehouse's gleaming white façade and wooden panels will attract any fervent media influencer or design enthusiast. It's also the world's first restaurant to receive a five-star rating from Green Star, Australia's trusted mark of quality for sustainable buildings. If I had to pick one mind-blowing element, it's their dramatic entrance: the eatery is built inside of a dune. The entire ground floor is buried underneath the sand, highlighting a small gap between the top of the dune and the dining area, which appears to be floating. Serving up fresh seafood (the rock lobster and king prawn tacos are amazing) with a relaxed vibe, this is the sweetest place to chill out and forget the world.

THE ASTOR THEATRE

Old-school movie palace

Corner of Chapel Street and Dandenong Road / +61 3 9510 1414
astortheatre.net.au / Open daily

The Astor Theatre brings the magic of 1930s cinema screenings to millennials. This Art Deco film center is Melbourne's last single screen cinema in continuous operation since its grand opening in 1936. With stalls and a dress circle, the vast space can seat 1,150 people at any one time and the grandeur of it all makes you forget you're about to watch a movie, not a musical or play. Soft golden curtains cover the giant screen before the movie begins, but once it comes to life, so does a state-of-the-art Dolby sound system. Take your pick from classics, cult darlings and select new releases.

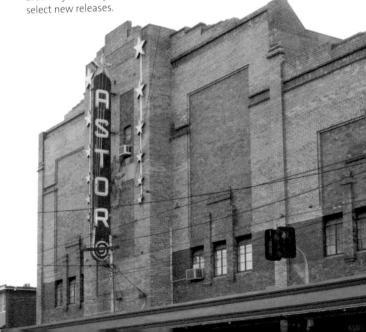

UNCLE

Modern Vietnamese fare

188 Carlisle Street (near Chapel Street) / +61 3 9041 2668
unclerestaurants.com.au / Open daily

Named after the much-used term of respect and endearment within Asian cultures, Uncle is a contemporary Vietnamese joint that brings a bit of fun, colorful dining to St Kilda's shores. There are intimate tables for two, space for large groups, bar seats and an outdoor courtyard for the kinds of warm evenings that beg to be passed under a string of pendant lights. Take your pick from a wide-ranging menu of items, such as lime-cured hapuka with coconut and pomegranate on a betel leaf, mini bowls of pho, oven-baked fish fillet and wok-tossed Wagyu brisket with steamed rice rolls, edamame, chili butter and bottarga (cured fish roe). The best part? The food is tasty and reasonably priced, which leaves me feeling extra satisfied.

gone road tripping

Spectacular drives and charming towns

GREAT OCEAN ROAD
MORNINGTON PENINSULA
YARRA VALLEY

Sprawling wineries, magnificent lookouts and secret back beaches... a quick hour's drive out of Melbourne's CBD will have you right in the heart of nature's finest. It's wise to plan your route early and decide whether you'll want to stay a night or two to soak in the incredible vistas the coast or wine region has to offer. Don't forget to check out the small towns on the way, because you never know what handmade treasures you'll come across.

If you only have time for one road trip, you'll want to head down to the winding coast along **Great Ocean Road** for the sublime views. I love to make my journey down to the famed 12 Apostles an adventure, stopping at towns like Torquay, Apollo Bay and Lorne. These beachside locations are terrific for picnicking, noshing on fish & chips and dipping your toes in the sand. Spa junkies, book in at Saltair Day Spa in advance for a wonderful experience. Their relaxation massage is something dreams are made of.

It's also worth it to drive in the other direction down **Mornington Peninsula** to Sorrento, Cape Schanck and Red Hill for a wider variety of activities. The Cups Estate and Foxey's Hangout are two of my preferred wineries out that way for their delightful produce and quality wines. You'll want to spend your entire afternoon taking in fresh air and rows of grapes. Or, pop in for a languid dip in natural thermal mineral waters at the Peninsula Hot Springs. There are over 20 bathing experiences including a cave pool, reflexology walk, Turkish hammam and cold plunge pool. Be sure to make your way to the hilltop pool for a breathtaking panorama at sunset.

Food and wine gourmands, the **Yarra Valley** wine region is right up your alley. Surrounded by lush rolling hills, there are heaps of wineries here for you to pick from. One of my favorite things to do in this area is to create a progressive lunch and check out a different venue for starter, main and dessert. Take your pick from Dominique Portet, Domaine Chandon, Stones of the Yarra Valley and Ezard. The best part? It's only a 45-minute drive from the city center.

elwood and brighton

Unlike the effervescent, party vibe of St Kilda, its neighbors Elwood and Brighton have a more settled, tranquil and residential feel. These beachside precincts line Melbourne's Port Phillip Bay and are dotted with stately homes that attract society's upper echelons. Brighton's renowned multihued bathing boxes reside out here along Dendy Street Beach and retain classic Victorian architectural elements with timber framing, weatherboards and corrugated iron roofs. From gastropubs to coffee spots to shopping galore, set aside a few hours here, if not an entire day – otherwise you'll feel rushed and unsatisfied. Elwood's Ormond Road is just as fun if you're after friendly neighborhood bookstores, gift shops or a smoothie run.

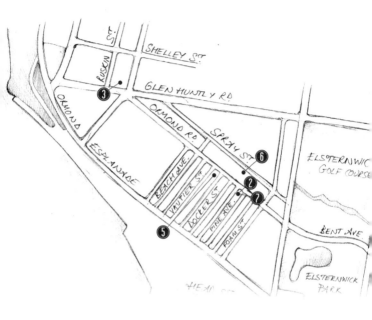

1 Church Street
2 Combi
3 Harrow & Eton
4 Jaggad
5 The Grumpy Swimmer
6 The Leaf Store
7 The Milton
8 The Pantry

CHURCH STREET

Village with a sunny disposition

churchstreetbrighton.com.au / Open daily

Apart from Chapel Street in South Yarra, I'd say Church Street in Brighton makes for one of the top shopping experiences in Melbourne. On a gloriously sunny day, it's picture perfect – rows of shops as far as the eye can see and people sitting out on the sidewalk enjoying coffees or beers. Check into Half Moon, a cool pub with rustic-chic, timber furnishings for charcuterie nibbles, tacos, fresh salads or large plates to share – there's nothing better than sitting out in their airy courtyard with a bunch of friends. Otherwise, grab a cuppa and superfood granola from the laidback Brighton Soul Espresso. Handworks Nouveau Paperie is a unique trove for stationery lovers, and I adore walking in here to the smell of candles and thumbing through the quirky coffee table books. Don't miss Il Migliore's pretty storefront, which will have you hooked with colorful boxes of gourmet biscuits, sweet treats and fancy hampers that make fantastic gifts.

COMBI

Hippie hole-in-the-wall

1/140 Ormond Road (near Docker Street) / +61 3 9531 0084
wearecombi.com.au / Open daily

This beach shack is rustic, fun and vibrant, and looks like it belongs on California's Venice Beach. Taking inspiration from their travels through Bali and Hawaii, owners Penny Loughnan and Anthony Baker's Combi is a healthy eating destination that even those who still eat gluten (like me) will go nuts over. Using only organic ingredients, their all-day menu features superfood smoothies, açaí bowls, raw zucchini spaghetti and scrumptious avocado toast topped with pumpkin seeds. There are even options to finish off on a sweet note – try their caramel slice or mango and passionfruit cheesecake.

HARROW & ETON

Good ol' homemade pies

61 Glenhuntly Road (near Broadway) / +61 4 1704 4655
harrowandeton.com.au / Closed Sunday and Monday

Owner Jo Ground is an extraordinary pie maker. Made entirely from scratch, all the meat is slow-cooked and simmered in a pot along with herbs and spices while she prepares her shortcrust pastry. From Catalan beef and peppered kangaroo to curried scallop, all her creations are melt-in-your-mouth delicious and have that lovely, homemade je ne sais quoi to them. My pick? The beef and Guinness, for its stunning balance in texture and flavor, and how it's so generously stuffed with double-smoked bacon, garlic and herbs.

JAGGAD

Fashion-forward sportswear

123 Church Street (near Male Street) / +61 3 9592 5986 / jaggad.com
Open daily

A stylish sports apparel brand owned by former AFL football players
Chris Judd and Steven Greene, Jaggad is a sartorial godsend for fitness
junkies looking for a new yoga or boot camp outfit. Their Brighton store
is expansive with lots of room to peruse items and navigate the racks.
Their multi-sport performance garments are cut from premium fabrics
and created by some of the world's most passionate designers, such as
Melbourne-based J'Aton Couture. I adore their compression leggings, which
are crafted to guarantee muscle control and provide a two-way stretch as
well as UV protection. It's like second skin whenever I exercise.

THE GRUMPY SWIMMER

Calling all bookworms

110 Ormond Road (near Docker Street) / +61 3 9525 7488
thegrumpyswimmer.com.au / Open daily

Its entrance may seem a tad unassuming, but once you step into this darling bookstore, you'll never want to leave. The Grumpy Swimmer is Elwood's neighborhood gem, stocking a range from cookbooks to travel guides to design and fashion titles. The front of the store is dedicated to gifts: there are divine-smelling candles and whimsically packaged Murphy & Daughters shea butter and goat milk soaps that are look like bon bons. Wander amongst neat shelves of fascinating reading material and a small children's section at the back. I love supporting local, and this bookstore is as local as it gets — and it definitely helps that their staff are some of the friendliest people on earth.

THE LEAF STORE

Healthy and wholesome grocer

111 Ormond Road (near Docker Street) / +61 3 9531 6542
theleafstore.com.au / Open daily

"If it's not good enough to feed my family, it's not good enough to be in my store," says owner Leon Mugavin. This dedicated man wakes up at 2am each day to pick the freshest produce for his village grocery store. With a focus on locally sourced products, The Leaf Store stocks a wide range of organic, gluten-free, dairy-free and vegetarian options alongside fresh deli items: think cheese-stuffed peppadews, charcuterie fixins, pâtés, rillettes and terrines, and glorious homemade dips. It's a well-curated supermarket for the health-conscious...and the en vogue couple who wishes to eat cleaner but maybe doesn't always succeed. You know you're getting the best of the best here, so it's well worth the trip.

THE MILTON

Industrial-chic bar with an open fire

134 Ormond Road (near Docker Street) / +61 3 9525 7346
themilton.co / Open daily

Modern industrialism is key in The Milton's clever fit out — featuring slanted roofs, wood-paneled ceilings, a variation of pendant lighting and exposed red-brick walls, there's heaps to take in when you enter this intimate eatery. The tapas-style plates, such as lamb kofta, are dished up with elegance and are all designed to pair beautifully with wine. I enjoy coming here on cold evenings, parking myself in front of the fire and sipping on my Ormond Old Fashioned, a smoky, bittersweet concoction that makes the world feel like an infinitely better place.

THE PANTRY

Modern Australian eats in a relaxed, beachside setting

1 Church Street (near St Andrews Street) / +61 3 9591 0393
pantry.com.au / Open daily

A bright daytime café that turns into a swish night-time diner, The Pantry is a buzzy, kid-friendly place where hip families retreat on the weekend. Try the linguine with king prawn, crab, garlic, chili, cherry tomato and olive oil for lip-smacking, hearty goodness — the flavors come together so delicately and you'll leave planning your next visit. They also do a mean beef and bacon burger with double cheese, tomato, onion and the works. The beef patty is juicy and tender and definitely well-worth the calories.

walking on sunshine

Expansive views, gorgeous lakes and dramatic geology

Victoria is home to diverse walking trails and hikes, offering city-dwellers a chance to venture out of the urban hubbub and take in the natural landscape. From riverside strolls to walks in the park to vertiginous climbs, there's so much beauty to take in – and the best part is, some of these trails are right in the city's backyard.

You'll never guess that such raw, pristine beauty exists so close to the city until you embark on the 12-kilometer (7.5-mile) **Fairfield Boathouse to Studley Boathouse** walk. Start at the Fairfield Boathouse and follow the dirt path until you reach Flying Fox Lookout, where you should take a moment to marvel at its panoramic views of vast wetlands, trees and flying foxes hanging from branches. Make your way to the calming Bellbird Picnic Area, and from there, hit up the meandering Yarra Boulevard before descending down the river and passing the iconic, wooden Kane's Bridge to Studley Boathouse. Enjoy a well-deserved break with a lovely selection of scones, clotted cream and tea.

Nothing feeds your soul like a walk by the water. The five-kilometer (3-mile) walk around the glittering **Albert Park Lake** boasts uninterrupted views of the CBD and is a serene path ideal for solo walks or long chats with your bestie. Pack a picnic or a book if you wish to stop along the way – and don't forget to keep an eye out for those stunning black swans.

ALBERT PARK LAKE

Whether it's taking a slow stroll in the **Royal Botanic Gardens** or a jog around the Tan Track that surrounds it, this verdant botanical gardens - which boasts over 10,000 floral species - is not one to be missed. It hosts over 10,000 floral species. Once you're done exercising, drop by at the Jardin Tan or The Kettle Black (see pg 63) across the road for an iced drink.

The wild, rugged beauty of the **Werribee Gorge Circuit Track** is certainly unparalleled. This 10-kilometer (6-mile) walk takes anything from two to three hours depending on how fast you travel, with impressive views of both the river and cliff faces of the gorge. Pack your bathers as you'll come across a few swimming holes, including the one at Needles Beach, along the way.

March your way up the steep, 1,000-step walk of the **Kokoda Track Memorial Walk** for a small taste of what Australian soldiers who followed the Kokoda Trail in Papua New Guinea during World War II went through. This three-kilometer (2-mile) ascent is a true workout, although I've seen people blitz through it like a piece of cake. I prefer taking it easy, breathing in the sweet mountainous air and delighting in the occasional run-in with a possum or Lyrebird.

ALBERT PARK LAKE
Along Lakeside Drive (near Albert Road Drive; South Melbourne)

FAIRFIELD BOATHOUSE TO STUDLEY PARK
Via Yarra Bend Road (Fairfield)

KOKODA TRACK MEMORIAL WALK
Lot 18 Belview Terrace (near School Track; Tremont)

ROYAL BOTANICAL GARDENS
Birdwood Avenue (near Domain Road; South Yarra)

WERRIBEE GORGE CIRCUIT TRACK
Starting point: Meikles Point Picnic Area
(along Myers Road; Ingliston)